Mobile Mastery: The Ultimate Guide to Successful Mobile Marketing Campaigns

B. Vincent

Published by RWG Publishing, 2023.

MOBILE MASTERY: THE ULTIMATE GUIDE TO SUCCESSFUL MOBILE MARKETING CAMPAIGNS

First edition. April 13, 2023.

Written by B. Vincent.

Also by B. Vincent

Affiliate Marketing
Affiliate Marketing
Affiliate Marketing

Standalone
Business Employee Discipline
Affiliate Recruiting
Business Layoffs & Firings
Business and Entrepreneur Guide
Business Remote Workforce
Career Transition
Project Management
Precision Targeting
Professional Development
Strategic Planning
Content Marketing
Imminent List Building
Getting Past GateKeepers
Banner Ads
Bookkeeping
Bridge Pages
Business Acquisition

Business Bogging
Business Communication Course
Marketing Automation
Better Meetings
Business Conflict Resolution
Business Culture Course
Conversion Optimization
Creative Solutions
Employee Recruitment
Startup Capital
Employee Incentives
Employee Mentoring
Followership
Servant Leadership
Human Resources
Team Building
Freelancing
Funnel Building
Geo Targeting
Goal Setting
Immanent List Building
Lead Generation
Leadership Course
Leadership Transition
Leadership vs Management
LinkedIn Ads
LinkedIn Marketing
Messenger Marketing
New Management
Newsfeed Ads
Search Ads
Online Learning
Sales Webinars

Side Hustles

Split Testing

Twitter Timeline Advertising

Earning Additional Income Through Side Hustles: Begin Earning Money Immediately

Making a Living Through Blogging: Earn Money Working From Home

Create Bonuses for Affiliate Marketing: Your Success Is Encompassed by Your Bonuses

Internet Marketing Success: The Most Effective Traffic-Driving Strategies

JV Recruiting: Joint Ventures Partnerships and Affiliates

Secrets to List Building

Step-by-Step Facebook Marketing: Discover How To Create A Strategy That Will Help You Grow Your Business

Banner Advertising: Traffic Can Be Boosted by Banner Ads

Affiliate Marketing

Improve Your Marketing Strategy with Internet Marketing

Outsourcing Helps You Save Time and Money

Choosing the Right Content and Marketing for Social Media

Make Products That Will Sell

Launching a Product for Affiliate Marketing

Pinterest as a Marketing Tool

Mobile Mastery: The Ultimate Guide to Successful Mobile Marketing Campaigns

Table of Contents

Chapter 1: Introduction to Mobile Marketing

Mobile devices have not only altered the ways in which we communicate and access information, but they have also brought about significant changes in the field of marketing. Mobile marketing is the practice of reaching customers through their mobile devices, such as smartphones and tablets, by utilizing a variety of marketing strategies, such as mobile apps, mobile websites, SMS marketing, social media, and even more. Mobile marketing is also referred to as mobile commerce. In the following chapter, we will go over the fundamentals of mobile marketing and discuss the reasons why it has become such an important part of any marketing strategy.

The Rapid Growth of Mobile Advertising

The rapid increase in the number of mobile devices being used all over the world is largely responsible for the rise of mobile marketing. According to Statista, the total number of smartphone users around the world is forecast to reach 3.8 billion in the year 2021, and it is anticipated that this number will continue to rise in the years to come. The increased use of mobile devices has resulted in a shift in the way in which customers interact with brands and has opened up fresh doors for businesses seeking to strengthen their connections with their target demographics.

Advantages of Utilizing Mobile Marketing

Including mobile marketing as part of your overall marketing strategy can confer a number of advantages to your business. To begin, mobile marketing enables you to communicate with members of your target audience whenever and wherever you choose. Customers are able to access your content from virtually any location thanks to the proliferation of mobile devices, which provides you with the opportunity to connect with them while you are on the move. Second, mobile marketing makes it possible to advertise to very specific demographics. Marketers are able to tailor their advertising to specific audiences by utilizing data such as geolocation and browsing history. This allows them to ensure that their message resonates with the appropriate people. In conclusion, mobile marketing has the potential to be very cost-efficient. Mobile marketing can often be more cost-effective than more traditional forms of advertising, such as print or television, making it possible for smaller businesses to compete successfully with larger ones.

Different Varieties of Mobile Marketing

There is a wide variety of mobile marketing strategies available for companies to choose from in order to communicate with their target demographic. The following are some of the most common:

Apps for mobile devices are software applications that have been developed specifically for use on mobile devices. It is possible for companies to create their own apps in order to provide customers with easier access to the products or services they offer.

Websites optimized for mobile devices Mobile websites offer a more streamlined browsing experience and are designed to display optimally on mobile devices. Mobile websites, in comparison to desktop websites, typically have fewer features, but they are designed to be more user-friendly on screens with a smaller resolution.

SMS marketing entails sending promotional messages to customers who have opted in to receive them via text message. This type of marketing is known as "text marketing." Marketing via text message (SMS) can be an extremely efficient method for running time-sensitive promotions or informing customers about brand new goods or services.

The use of social media platforms such as Facebook, Instagram, and Twitter can be effective ways to communicate with customers who access their devices through mobile browsers. Businesses are able to develop relationships with their target audience and increase traffic to their website by producing content that is compelling and actively engaging with their followers.

The display of advertisements on mobile devices, most frequently by means of mobile applications or mobile websites, is what is referred to as mobile advertising. Mobile ads can be extremely targeted, enabling marketers to communicate with specific audiences using content that is pertinent to their needs.

The Obstacles Faced by Mobile Marketing

Mobile marketing presents a number of challenges in addition to its many opportunities. These challenges should be taken into consideration. One of the most difficult obstacles is the fragmentation that exists within the mobile market. Because there are so many different kinds of devices and operating systems, it can be challenging to make sure that your content is optimized for all of the different kinds of devices. Because of the small screen size of mobile devices, it can be difficult to communicate complicated ideas or design visually appealing advertisements. This is another one of the challenges that mobile marketers face. Last but not least, the ever-increasing prevalence of ad-blocking software on mobile devices can make it challenging to connect with customers through conventional channels of advertising.

Conclusion

Mobile marketing is a rapidly developing field that offers many benefits to businesses that are looking to connect with their audience. In conclusion, mobile marketing is a field that is rapidly growing. You will be able to reach customers at any time and in any location by incorporating mobile marketing techniques into your overall marketing strategy. Furthermore, you will be able to tailor your messaging to the specific audiences you are targeting. However, it is essential to keep in mind the difficulties that are associated with mobile marketing. These difficulties include the fragmentation of the market as well as the restricted screen size of mobile devices. Mobile marketing has the potential to be an effective method of propelling business growth and achieving marketing goals, provided that it is carefully planned and carried out. In the following chapters, we will delve into a more in-depth discussion of the various forms of mobile marketing, such as mobile advertising, mobile marketing via social media, mobile marketing via SMS, and mobile marketing via mobile apps and mobile websites. We will also look at best practices for developing a mobile marketing strategy, such as how to make mobile content that is compelling, how to optimize for mobile SEO, and how to measure the return on investment of your campaigns. Understanding mobile marketing is absolutely necessary in order to maintain a competitive edge in the modern-day digital landscape, regardless of whether you run a small business or work in the marketing industry.

Chapter 2: The Evolution of Mobile Marketing

Since 1973, when the first mobile phone was introduced to the world, there has been a significant advancement in the field of mobile marketing. The evolution of mobile technology has presented new opportunities for marketers to connect with their target audience. The first SMS message was sent in 1992, and the first iPhone was released in 2007. Both of these dates mark significant milestones in the history of mobile technology. In this chapter, we will delve into the past of mobile marketing and examine how it has progressed over the years to become the effective instrument that it is today.

Infancy of Mobile Advertising and Marketing

Text message marketing was one of the earliest forms of mobile marketing and can be traced back to the early 2000s, when the first mobile marketing campaigns were run. The very first short message service (SMS) transmission took place in 1992, but it wasn't until the early 2000s that companies started experimenting with sending marketing messages to customers via text message. Coca-Cola was one of the first companies to launch a text message marketing campaign in 2003. The campaign encouraged customers to text in for a chance to win prizes.

Nevertheless, early mobile marketing campaigns were constrained by the technology that was available at the time. It was expensive to send a text message using a mobile phone, which was one of the reasons why mobile phones were still relatively simple. As a direct consequence of this, early mobile marketing campaigns concentrated primarily on elevating brand recognition rather than on actively driving sales.

The Ascent of the Mobile Phone

The introduction of the very first iPhone in 2007 was a pivotal moment in the development of mobile marketing, as it marked the beginning of a new era. The introduction of the iPhone, which was the first smartphone to feature a touch screen, internet connectivity, and the capability to download applications, was a significant step forward for the mobile industry.

Mobile marketing has progressed beyond the use of straightforward text message campaigns since the proliferation of smartphones. It is now possible for businesses to develop mobile apps and mobile websites in order to provide customers with experiences that are more immersive and engaging. Apps designed specifically for mobile devices, in particular, have emerged as a potent instrument for use by businesses that seek to connect with their audience.

The Accelerating Development of Mobile Advertising

The rise in the use of smartphones coincided with the beginning of an explosion in mobile advertising. Just $2.2 billion was spent globally on mobile advertising in 2010, according to estimates. By the year 2020, that figure had increased to more than 240 billion dollars.

Mobile advertising has a number of benefits to offer in comparison to more traditional advertising channels. It gives companies the ability to target specific audiences based on factors such as location, browsing history, and other demographic data. Mobile advertisements are also capable of providing a high level of engagement by incorporating elements of interactivity such as videos and games.

The widespread adoption of various social media platforms.

The use of social media platforms such as Facebook, Instagram, and Twitter has developed into an essential component of mobile marketing. Businesses have the opportunity to reach a large audience that is actively engaged through the use of social media advertising because millions of users access social media on their mobile devices.

Additionally, social media platforms provide companies with the opportunity to cultivate relationships with their target audience through consistent engagement and the production of content. Businesses have the ability to raise consumer awareness of their brands, increase traffic to their websites, and generate leads and sales by establishing a robust presence on social media.

The Surging Popularity of Mobile Video

As the processing power of mobile devices has increased, mobile video has emerged as one of the most engaging forms of content that can be found on mobile devices. A new study found that as of right now, mobile video accounts for sixty percent of all video views all over the world.

Businesses can benefit in a variety of ways from mobile video's presence. It gives them the ability to tell stories that are interesting and captivating, to demonstrate their goods or services, and to connect with their audience on a more personal level. Mobile video can also be easily shared with others, which expands the audience that is exposed to your message.

The Prospects for Mobile Marketing in the Future

It appears that mobile marketing has a prosperous future ahead of it as technology continues to advance. Some companies are already using up-and-coming technologies such as augmented reality and virtual reality to provide their customers with more immersive experiences. Personalizing mobile marketing messages and improving targeting are also two goals that are being pursued with the help of artificial intelligence and machine learning.

The proliferation of 5G networks will also have a sizeable influence on mobile marketing due to their anticipated significant effects. The introduction of 5G will make it possible for businesses to create mobile experiences that are more immersive and interactive than ever before, from live video streaming to augmented reality and virtual reality applications.

Conclusion

In conclusion, the development of mobile marketing has been molded by the progression of technology, beginning with the introduction of text messaging and continuing with the rise of smartphones and social media. Mobile marketing has evolved into a potent instrument that companies can use to connect with their target audience. It provides highly targeted advertising, engaging content, and marketing campaigns that are efficient in terms of cost.

Emerging technologies such as augmented reality and virtual reality as well as artificial intelligence are set to transform the way in which businesses connect with their target audience, which bodes well for the future of mobile marketing. Businesses that invest in mobile marketing are likely to see continued growth and success in the years to come as mobile devices continue to play an increasingly important role in our lives. This is because mobile devices continue to play an increasingly important role in our lives. In the following chapters, we will delve deeper into the various types of mobile marketing techniques and explore how businesses can create successful mobile marketing campaigns using mobile marketing.

Chapter 3: Understanding Your Mobile Audience

Understanding your mobile audience is absolutely necessary if you want to run mobile marketing campaigns that are successful. Mobile devices are extremely personal, and users expect content to be tailored to their specific needs and interests. You will be able to create targeted marketing campaigns that resonate with your audience if you have a thorough understanding of the needs, preferences, and behaviors of your audience. In this chapter, we will discuss how to understand your mobile audience in order to better cater your mobile marketing strategy to the requirements that they have.

The demographics of people who use mobile devices

Establishing the demographics of your mobile audience is the first step in developing an understanding of that audience. A recent report found that the majority of people who use mobile devices are between the ages of 18 and 34, and that slightly more men than women use mobile devices. Nevertheless, the age distribution of mobile users and the gender split of mobile users can differ depending on the business sector, the product or service being marketed, and the geographic location of your audience.

The level of income, the level of education, and the occupation are also important demographic factors to take into consideration. If you have a better understanding of these demographic factors, you will be able to better tailor your messaging and produce more successful mobile marketing campaigns.

Preferences and Behaviors Regarding Mobile Devices

In addition to demographic factors, it is essential to have a solid understanding of the mobile behaviors and preferences of your target audience. To give one example, when using their mobile devices, do they favor mobile apps or mobile websites? Do they typically access your content through a particular kind of device, like a smartphone or a tablet computer? By gaining an understanding of these preferences, you can better adapt your mobile marketing strategy to meet the requirements of your audience.

The time of day during which your audience is most active on mobile devices is another factor that is very important to take into consideration. For instance, if the majority of your audience consists of young professionals, they might be more likely to engage with your content while they are traveling to and from work in the morning and evening. By gaining an understanding of these patterns, you will be able to time the delivery of your mobile marketing campaigns to coincide with the times during which your audience is most likely to be engaged.

Mobile User Experience

When developing strategies for mobile marketing, another essential component to take into consideration is the mobile user experience. Mobile devices typically have more compact displays than desktop computers, so users anticipate content that has been formatted specifically for mobile viewing. Engaging your audience requires you to have a website or app that is optimized for mobile use, straightforward in its navigation, and quick to load.

Your mobile marketing campaigns should also give careful consideration to how the end user will experience them. For instance, in regards to clarity and ease of comprehension, how would you rate your call-to-action? Are your mobile ads optimized for mobile devices, and do they provide an experience that is engaging enough to hold the attention of your target audience? You can increase engagement and conversions by ensuring that mobile users have a positive experience with your app.

Data and Analytics for Mobile Devices

It is important to collect and analyze data regarding the preferences and behaviors of your mobile audience in order to gain a deeper understanding of that audience. Mobile analytics tools such as Google

Analytics and Flurry Analytics can provide valuable insights into the mobile behavior of your audience. These insights can include how your audience interacts with your website or app, the types of content they engage with, and the devices they use.

You can identify trends and patterns in the mobile behavior of your audience by analyzing this data, and you can then use this information to improve your mobile marketing campaigns by putting this information to use. For instance, if you find that a certain category of content is more well-liked by your audience, you could produce more of that category of content in order to engage your audience in a more meaningful way.

Conclusion

In conclusion, it is essential to develop successful mobile marketing campaigns by first gaining an understanding of the mobile audience you are targeting. You will be able to customize your mobile marketing strategy to meet the requirements and preferences of your target audience if you first determine their demographics, mobile behaviors, preferences, and user experiences. You will be able to create more successful campaigns, as well as improve engagement and conversions, if you make use of mobile data and analytics, which can provide valuable insights into the behavior of your audience. In the following chapters, we will investigate the various strategies of mobile marketing and discuss how to apply them in order to effectively reach and engage your audience.

Chapter 4: Building Your Mobile Marketing Strategy

In order to construct a mobile marketing strategy that is effective, careful planning and execution are required. Your overall marketing goals should be aligned with your mobile marketing strategy, and your mobile marketing strategy should be tailored to the needs and preferences of your mobile audience. In this chapter, we will discuss how to construct a mobile marketing strategy that will assist you in effectively reaching and engaging your audience in order to achieve your marketing goals.

Establishing Objectives for Your Mobile Marketing

Choosing what you want to achieve with your mobile marketing strategy is the first thing you need to do. What are you hoping to accomplish with the campaigns you run for mobile marketing? Increasing website traffic is one of the most common objectives, along with generating leads or sales, improving customer engagement and retention, building brand awareness, and so on.

You will be able to create a mobile marketing strategy that is focused and targeted if you define your goals first. This will allow you to evaluate how well your strategy is working and make adjustments as necessary.

Establishing Who Your Ideal Customers Are

After you have decided what you want to accomplish, the next step is to determine who your audience will be. Who do you hope to engage with the mobile marketing campaigns that you are running? What are some of their preferences, as well as their mobile behavior and demographic characteristics?

Your ability to create mobile marketing campaigns that resonate with your target audience, thereby increasing engagement and conversions, is directly proportional to your understanding of that audience. You can also make use of this information to customize your messaging and produce content that is specific to your audience and relevant to their needs by using the information.

Choosing the Right Channels for Your Mobile Marketing

There is a wide variety of mobile marketing channels available, and some of these channels include mobile apps, mobile websites, SMS marketing, social media marketing, and mobile advertising. Each channel has a specific set of benefits and drawbacks, and the one that will be most appropriate for your company will be the one that best fits your objectives, target demographic, and financial constraints.

Apps for mobile devices, for instance, are capable of providing users with a highly engaging and individualized experience. However, their development can be costly, and they require regular upkeep and modifications after they are implemented. On the other hand, mobile websites are more accessible and affordable, but they might not offer the same level of engagement as mobile apps.

Marketing via text message (SMS) can be an extremely efficient method for running time-sensitive promotions or informing customers about brand new goods or services. Platforms for social media such as Facebook and Instagram can be extremely useful instruments for fostering relationships with an audience as well as attracting visitors to a website. Mobile advertising has the potential to be highly engaging and targeted, but it can also be quite pricey.

You will be able to effectively reach your audience and accomplish your marketing goals if you choose the appropriate channels for your mobile marketing.

Developing Content for Mobile Devices That Is Captivating

It is essential to create compelling content for mobile devices if you wish to engage your audience and realize your marketing objectives. Mobile devices typically have more compact displays than desktop computers, so users anticipate content that has been formatted specifically for mobile viewing.

When developing content for mobile devices, it is essential to keep the interface uncomplicated and user-friendly at all times. To get the attention of your target audience, craft messages that are straightforward and to the point, and include visual components such as pictures and videos. Think about the experience of using your product, and make sure that it's optimized for viewing on mobile devices.

Evaluation of Your Performance

It is essential to the success of your mobile marketing strategy that you measure the results of your efforts. You will be able to determine what aspects of your strategy are successful and which require modification if you keep track of your performance and analyze the data.

Mobile analytics tools such as Google Analytics or Flurry Analytics can provide valuable insights into your mobile marketing campaigns, including metrics such as website traffic, engagement, and conversions. These tools can also provide valuable insights into your mobile marketing campaigns. You will be able to identify areas in which you need to improve as well as make decisions based on the data in order to optimize your campaigns if you analyze this data.

Conclusion

In conclusion, developing a strategy for effective mobile marketing requires both careful planning and deliberate implementation. You can create mobile marketing campaigns that engage your audience and help you achieve your marketing goals if you define your goals, determine your target audience, select the appropriate mobile marketing channels, develop compelling mobile content, and measure your results. In the following chapters, we will investigate the numerous approaches to mobile marketing that exist, as well as discuss how to integrate these approaches into an efficient overall strategy for mobile marketing.

Chapter 5: Developing Your Mobile Brand

Building a reputable mobile brand is absolutely necessary if you want your mobile marketing strategy to be successful. A powerful mobile brand has the potential to increase customer loyalty, build trust, and differentiate your company from those of your competitors. In this chapter, we will discuss how to build a powerful mobile brand and then use that brand to create a powerful presence in the mobile space.

Establishing the Identity of Your Brand

Establishing your brand's identity is the first thing you should do when developing your mobile brand. Your company's name, as well as its colors, logo, and any messages associated with the brand, make up its identity. Your mobile app, mobile website, and mobile advertising should all reflect a unified and coherent representation of your brand identity throughout the entirety of your mobile marketing efforts.

Your company's values and mission statement should be reflected in your brand identity, and it should also be tailored to meet the requirements and preferences of your target audience. Your communication should be straightforward, succinct, and simple to comprehend, and the visuals you use should be engaging and aesthetically pleasing.

Constructing a Website and Mobile Application That Are Both Mobile-Friendly

In order to construct a powerful mobile brand, it is necessary to develop a website and an application that are compatible with mobile devices. Both your mobile website and app should have an intuitive navigation structure and be formatted appropriately for viewing on mobile devices. Your website and app should also reflect your brand identity by utilizing branding and messaging that is consistent throughout both platforms.

Your website and app should be designed with your target audience in mind, providing a personalized experience that satisfies their requirements and preferences as much as possible. To boost user engagement and offer them a one-of-a-kind experience, you might want to think about incorporating interactive elements like videos and games into your website.

Using Mobile Content to Capture the Attention of Your Audience

The ability to keep your audience interested through the use of mobile content is an essential element in developing a powerful mobile brand. Your mobile content should be tailored to the specific requirements and preferences of your target audience, while also maintaining the integrity of your brand identity. To boost user engagement and deliver a more tailored experience to each individual user, you might want to think about integrating features such as user-generated content, social media integration, and push notifications.

Engaging your audience with mobile content can also be accomplished with the help of powerful tools provided by social media platforms such as Facebook, Instagram, and Twitter. You can raise consumers' awareness of your brand and forge stronger connections with them by establishing a robust social media presence, using it on a regular basis, and publishing content that is both pertinent and engaging.

Assessing the Performance of Your Brand

When it comes to developing a powerful mobile brand, measuring the success of your brand is absolutely necessary. You can determine what aspects of your brand strategy are successful and what aspects are not by monitoring metrics such as brand awareness, customer loyalty, and engagement. You can then adjust your brand strategy to reflect your findings.

Mobile analytics tools such as Google Analytics or Flurry Analytics can provide valuable insights into the performance of your brand, including metrics such as website traffic, engagement, and conversions. These tools can also provide valuable insights into the performance of mobile apps. You will be able to identify areas in which you need to improve as well as make decisions based on the data in order to optimize your brand strategy if you analyze this data.

Creating a Group of Mobile Users as a Community

When it comes to developing a powerful mobile brand, one of the most important things to do is to cultivate a user community. You can strengthen the loyalty of your customers and build a positive reputation for your brand by cultivating relationships with the people who use your mobile app and by offering them individualized experiences.

To foster a sense of community among your mobile users, you might want to think about incorporating features such as user-generated content, integration with social media, and push notifications. You can build a strong community of loyal mobile users by responding to feedback from customers and providing exceptional customer service. Both of these strategies can help you.

Conclusion

In conclusion, if you want your mobile marketing strategy to be successful, building a solid mobile brand is absolutely necessary. You can create a strong mobile presence that resonates with your target audience by defining your brand identity, developing a mobile-friendly website and app, engaging your audience with mobile content, measuring the success of your brand, and building a community of mobile users. In the following chapters, we will investigate the numerous approaches to mobile marketing that are available, as well as discuss how to make the most of each strategy when developing your mobile brand.

Chapter 6: Creating Effective Mobile Advertisements

Mobile advertising is a powerful tool that companies can use to reach and engage the audience they are trying to reach. However, because more people are using ad-blocking software and there is more competition, it is essential to develop mobile advertisements that are memorable to your target audience and that differentiate themselves from the crowd. In this chapter, we will discuss how to effectively create advertisements for mobile devices that can drive engagement as well as conversions.

Establishing Objectives for Your Mobile Advertising

Establishing your advertising objectives is the initial step in the process of developing successful mobile advertisements. What are you hoping to accomplish with the mobile advertising campaigns you are running? Increasing brand awareness, generating leads or sales, improving customer engagement and retention, and driving traffic to a website are some common goals.

You will be able to create mobile advertising campaigns that are focused and targeted if you first define your goals. This will allow you to measure how successful your campaigns are and adjust your strategy as necessary.

How to Determine Which Advertising Format Is Best

There is a wide variety of options available to choose from when it comes to the format of mobile advertisements, such as banner ads, interstitial ads, video ads, native ads, and many more. The format of the advertisement that is most effective for your company will be determined by your business's goals, its intended audience, and its available funds.

If you want to increase brand awareness and drive traffic to your website, banner ads, for example, can be very effective. However, they may not be as engaging as other types of advertisements. Interstitial advertisements, on the other hand, have the potential to be highly engaging; however, users may find them to be intrusive.

Video advertisements have the potential to be extremely engaging and productive when it comes to telling a story and showcasing products or services. Native advertisements are advertisements that are designed to blend in with the content of a website or app. This provides the user with a more natural and less disruptive experience.

You'll be able to create mobile advertisements that resonate with your audience and accomplish your advertising goals if you select the appropriate ad format when you're working on your ads.

Developing Ad Content That Is Compelling

It is essential to create advertising content that is compelling if you want to engage your audience and drive conversions. Mobile devices typically have more compact displays than desktop computers, so users anticipate content that has been formatted specifically for mobile viewing.

When developing content for mobile advertisements, it is critical to keep the messaging straightforward and easy to comprehend. To get the attention of your target audience, craft messages that are straightforward and to the point, and include visual components such as pictures and videos. Take into account the experience of the user and check to see that the content of your ads can be viewed effectively on mobile devices.

Adapting Your Ads to Fit the Needs of Your Customers

It is essential to tailor your advertisements to your target audience in order to create effective mobile advertisements. Mobile devices are extremely personal, and users expect content to be tailored to their specific needs and interests.

Think about directing your advertisements toward particular subsets of the audience based on demographic characteristics such as age, gender, and location. You can also target your advertisements based on user behavior, such as a user's browsing history or their time spent using an application.

You can create more effective mobile advertisements that resonate with your audience, drive engagement, and convert more customers if you tailor your ads to your audience and make them more relevant to them.

Assessing the Effectiveness of Your Advertisements

It is essential to the success of your mobile advertising campaigns that you measure the performance of your advertisements. You can determine what aspects of your advertising strategy are successful and what aspects are not by monitoring metrics such as the number of ad impressions, clicks, and conversions. You can then adapt your strategy accordingly.

Mobile advertising platforms such as Google Ads and Facebook Ads provide valuable insights into the performance of your ads. These insights can be gleaned from metrics such as click-through rate, cost-per-click, and conversion rate. You will be able to identify areas in which you need to improve and make decisions based on the data in order to maximize the effectiveness of your mobile advertising campaigns if you analyze this data.

Conclusion

In conclusion, in order to create mobile advertisements that are effective, careful planning and implementation are required. You can create mobile advertisements that resonate with your target audience and achieve your advertising goals if you first define your advertising goals, then select the appropriate ad format, then create compelling ad content, then tailor your ads to your audience, and finally measure the performance of your ads. In the following chapters, we will investigate the various approaches to mobile marketing that are available, as well as discuss how to put these approaches to use in order to develop mobile advertising campaigns that are effective.

Chapter 7: Mobile App Marketing 101

Apps for mobile devices provide businesses with a potent instrument for engaging their target audience and driving conversions. However, given the availability of millions of apps, it is essential to have a solid mobile app marketing strategy in order to distinguish oneself from the competition and attract users. In this chapter, we will discuss how to develop a mobile app marketing strategy for your company that will increase the number of app installations and keep your target audience interested.

Establishing Your App Marketing Objectives

Establishing your app marketing objectives is the first thing you need to do in order to build a successful mobile app marketing strategy. What do you hope to accomplish with the marketing campaigns you run for your app? Increasing app installs, improving app engagement and retention, and driving in-app purchases are all common goals. Other goals include improving app retention rates.

You will be able to create a mobile app marketing strategy that is focused and targeted if you define your goals first. This will allow you to measure how well your strategy is working and make adjustments as necessary.

Getting the Most Out of Your App Store Listing

It is absolutely necessary to optimize your app store listing in order to drive app installs and engagement. Your listing in the app store ought to be user-friendly and search engine optimized for maximum exposure. Your app listing ought to also reflect the identity of your brand, with branding and messaging that are consistent throughout.

Your app listing ought to include compelling visuals such as screenshots and videos that demonstrate the features and benefits of your app. When describing the value proposition and benefits of your app, use messaging that is crystal clear and to the point. Additionally, consider incorporating social proof such as user ratings and reviews to increase credibility and trust.

Using Social Media to Promote Your Application

It is a powerful method for reaching and engaging your audience to promote your app on social media platforms. Promoting your app on social media platforms such as Facebook, Instagram, and Twitter is one of the most efficient and cost-effective ways to cultivate relationships with your target audience.

You should think about using ads on social media to reach the audience you want and to drive app installs. You can also create social media posts and stories to highlight the features and benefits of your app, as well as provide tips and tutorials on how to use your app.

Engaging Your App Users

It is absolutely necessary to engage your app's users in order to increase app retention and in-app purchases. Think about integrating features such as push notifications, in-app messaging, and loyalty programs into your app in order to engage your users and encourage them to use it repeatedly.

It is possible for push notifications to be an extremely efficient tool for increasing app engagement and delivering highly personalized experiences to users. Users can be encouraged to use your app and make in-app purchases by offering loyalty programs and providing support through in-app messaging. Support and questions from users can be answered through in-app messaging.

Assessing the Effectiveness of Your Application's Marketing

It is absolutely essential to the success of your mobile app marketing strategy that you measure the performance of your app marketing. You can determine what is successful and what is not in your app marketing strategy by tracking metrics such as the number of app installs, the level of engagement users have with the app, and the percentage of users who continue to use the app.

Mobile app analytics tools such as Google Analytics for Firebase or Flurry Analytics can give you valuable insights into the performance of your app. These insights can include metrics such as user behavior, engagement, and conversions. You will be able to identify areas in which you need to improve and make decisions based on the data in order to maximize the effectiveness of your app marketing campaigns if you analyze this data.

Conclusion

In conclusion, developing a strategy for marketing a mobile app that is successful requires both careful planning and precise execution. You can create a mobile app marketing strategy that drives installs and engagement by first defining the goals you want to achieve with your app marketing, then optimizing your app store listing, promoting your app on social media, engaging the users of your app, and measuring how well your app marketing is working. In the following chapters, we will investigate the numerous approaches to mobile marketing that are available, as well as discuss how to put these approaches to work in order to develop successful marketing campaigns for mobile apps.

Chapter 8: Mobile Search Engine Optimization (SEO)

The process of optimizing your website and its content for mobile search engines such as Google, Bing, and Yahoo is referred to as mobile search engine optimization (SEO) in its abbreviated form. Because mobile devices now account for more than half of all website traffic, search engine optimization (SEO) for mobile platforms is absolutely necessary for companies that want to reach and engage their target audience. We will discuss how to optimize your website and its content for mobile search engines in this chapter.

Understanding the Factors That Affect the Ranking of Mobile Search Engines

It is imperative that you have a solid understanding of the ranking factors that are utilized by search engines in the process of determining search rankings in order to successfully optimize your website for mobile search engines. The following are some factors that affect mobile search engine rankings:

The design of your website should be mobile-friendly, meaning that it is optimized for use on mobile devices and features a responsive layout that adapts to a variety of screen sizes.

Speed of the page: Your website should be able to load quickly on mobile devices, with quick page load times that make the user experience better.

Your content should be pertinent to the user's search query and offer something of value to the user in order to be considered relevant.

Keywords: To improve your search rankings, use keywords that are relevant to both the content you are creating and the audience you are aiming to attract.

Backlinks: An increase in the number of high-quality backlinks pointing to your website from other authoritative websites can help your site move up in the search rankings.

Adapting Your Website to Work Properly on Mobile Devices

It is essential for the success of mobile search engine optimization that your website be optimized for mobile devices. Your website ought to have simple navigation and ought to be optimized for viewing on mobile devices.

Make use of responsive design to make sure that your website is adaptable to a variety of screen sizes and offers a streamlined experience for its visitors. To keep the interest of your audience, use messaging that is both clear and succinct, and incorporate visual elements such as pictures and videos.

Adapting Your Content to Work Properly on Mobile Devices

It is essential for the success of your mobile search engine optimization to optimize your content for mobile devices. Your content ought to be simple to read and navigate on a mobile device, with messaging that is both clear and succinct and visuals that are interesting to look at.

To make your content more readable and scannable, you might want to think about incorporating elements such as headings, bullet points, and short paragraphs. Make use of images and videos to break up large blocks of text and provide a more visually appealing experience for the people who are utilizing your website.

Making Use of Keywords and Backlinks for Mobile Search Engine Optimization

It is absolutely necessary to make use of keywords and backlinks in order to improve your rankings in mobile search engines. Make use of keywords that are pertinent to both the content you are creating and the audience you are trying to attract, and then incorporate those keywords into your content as well as your meta tags.

Your mobile website's search engine rankings can also be improved by obtaining backlinks from other authoritative websites that are of a high quality. Think about forming strategic alliances with other companies operating in your sector and producing content that those companies can link to.

Assessing the Results of Your Mobile Search Engine Optimization

It is absolutely necessary to measure the performance of your mobile SEO in order to raise your search rankings and attract more visitors to your website. Tracking metrics such as website traffic, user engagement, and conversions can be accomplished with the help of mobile analytics tools such as Google Analytics.

You will be able to identify areas in which you need to improve and make decisions based on the collected data in order to make your mobile SEO strategy as effective as possible.

Conclusion

In conclusion, mobile search engine optimization is critical for companies to implement if they want to reach and engage their target audience. You can improve your search rankings and drive traffic to your website by becoming familiar with the factors that mobile search engines use to determine ranking positions, optimizing your website and its content for mobile devices, making use of keywords and backlinks, and monitoring how well your mobile SEO is working. In the following chapters, we will investigate the numerous approaches to mobile marketing that are available, as well as discuss how to utilize these approaches most effectively for mobile search engine optimization.

Chapter 9: The Power of Mobile Video Marketing

The use of mobile video marketing is an effective method for companies to communicate with and interact with their target audience. Mobile video has emerged as an indispensable component of the marketing mix in recent years, thanks to the proliferation of mobile technology and social media platforms. In this chapter, we will discuss how to effectively create mobile video marketing campaigns that drive engagement and conversions. These campaigns will be driven by mobile devices.

Comprehending the Influence That Mobile Video Can Have

Mobile video, which is both highly engaging and immersive, is a form of content that has the potential to effectively communicate one's message while also entrancing one's audience. Mobile video has emerged as an essential component of a successful marketing strategy for companies of all sizes, thanks to the proliferation of mobile-friendly social media platforms such as TikTok, Instagram, and YouTube.

Mobile video can be used for a wide variety of purposes, including but not limited to the telling of stories, the showcasing of products or services, the provision of tutorials and educational content, and more. You can increase brand awareness, drive engagement with your audience, and ultimately drive conversions if you create compelling video content that resonates with your target demographic.

Developing Beneficial Content for Mobile Video Devices

It is absolutely necessary to produce engaging mobile video content if you want to drive conversions and keep your audience interested. When developing content for mobile video, it is essential to keep the videos brief and to the point, with a message that is understandable and that will resonate with the target audience.

In order to effectively convey your message and capture the attention of your audience, you should make use of techniques such as compelling visuals, music, and storytelling. If you want to boost engagement and give your users a more individualized experience, you should think about incorporating interactive elements into your website. Some examples of these elements include polls, quizzes, and calls to action.

How to Get the Most Out of Your Mobile Videos on All Available Platforms

It is essential to optimize your mobile video for various platforms if you want to reach and engage the audience you are trying to attract. Because the various social media platforms each have their own unique requirements and parameters for videos, it is essential that your videos be adapted to meet those demands.

Take into consideration the creation of vertical videos for platforms such as TikTok and Instagram, which are designed specifically for viewing on mobile devices. Consider producing longer-form videos that offer more in-depth content and storytelling for platforms such as YouTube.

Getting Social Media Users to Watch Your Mobile Videos

It is imperative that you spread the word about your mobile video on social media in order to reach and engage your target audience. The use of social media platforms such as Facebook, Instagram, and Twitter offers a way to promote your videos in a manner that is both efficient and cost-effective, and to cultivate relationships with your audience.

You should think about using ads on social media to reach the audience you want and to drive video views. You can also create posts and stories on social media to promote the content of your videos and provide context and background information.

Assessing the Capabilities of Your Mobile Video Device

It is essential to measure the performance of your mobile video content if you want your mobile video marketing campaigns to be successful. You'll be able to determine what aspects of your video marketing strategy are successful and what aspects need improvement if you track metrics such as the number of video views, the amount of engagement, and the number of conversions.

Mobile video analytics tools such as YouTube Analytics or Instagram Insights can provide valuable insights into the performance of your video, including metrics such as demographics of the audience, engagement with the video, and retention of the video. You will be able to identify areas in which you need to improve as well as make decisions driven by the data in order to optimize your video marketing campaigns if you analyze this data.

Conclusion

To summarize, mobile video marketing is an effective method for businesses to connect with and interact with their target audience. You can create successful mobile video marketing campaigns that drive engagement and conversions by producing mobile video content that is effective, optimizing your videos for a variety of platforms, promoting your videos on social media, and measuring the performance of your videos. In the following chapters, we will investigate the various approaches to mobile marketing that are available, as well as discuss how to apply these approaches successfully to mobile video marketing.

Chapter 10: How to Use SMS Marketing for Optimal Results

SMS marketing is an effective method for companies to communicate with and engage their target audience. SMS marketing can be an effective way to drive conversions and build relationships with your customers because of the high open and response rates of SMS messages. In this chapter, we will discuss the best ways to use SMS marketing to get the most out of your efforts.

Understanding SMS Marketing

SMS marketing entails sending text messages to a database of subscribers who have opted-in to receive messages from your company. These subscribers have previously provided their contact information. You can use short message service (SMS) to communicate with your audience about important information, including updates, promotional offers, and more.

SMS messages offer a high level of personalization, in addition to high open and response rates; as a result, they are a useful tool for businesses that want to engage their audience. However, it is essential to use SMS marketing in a responsible manner and to ensure that the messages you send to your subscribers offer something of value to them.

Developing Your Short Message Service Marketing List

The development of your SMS marketing list is absolutely necessary for the accomplishment of your SMS marketing objectives. You should only send SMS messages to subscribers who have opted in to receive messages from your company. This is the only group of people to whom you should send SMS messages.

To collect phone numbers from interested subscribers, you might want to put opt-in forms on your website or social media platforms and promote them there. You can also encourage sign-ups by offering incentives such as discounts or content that is only accessible to subscribers.

Constructing Text Messages That Are Effective

It is essential to develop an audience engagement strategy that includes the creation of effective SMS messages in order to drive conversions. When developing SMS messages, it is essential to keep them brief and to the point, with a message that is easy to understand and that offers something of value to the subscribers.

To get the attention of your target audience, craft messages that are straightforward and to the point, and include visual components such as images and emojis. If you want to boost engagement and increase conversions, you should think about incorporating interactive elements into your content such as polls, surveys, and calls to action.

When to Send Your Text Messages and Why

When it comes to the success of your SMS marketing campaigns, timing your messages correctly is of the utmost importance. Sending SMS messages to your audience at a time that is convenient for them and offers them something of value should be your top priority.

You might want to think about sending messages during business hours, and you should try to avoid sending messages too early in the morning or too late at night. In addition, there are data analytics tools that can be used to determine the optimal times to send messages to an audience based on the actions and preferences of that audience.

Evaluation of the Effectiveness of Your SMS Marketing

It is essential to the success of your SMS marketing campaigns that you measure the effectiveness of your SMS marketing efforts. You can determine what aspects of your SMS marketing strategy are successful and what aspects are not by tracking metrics such as the number of messages delivered, the number of messages opened, and the number of responses received.

SMS marketing platforms such as Twilio and EZ Texting give you valuable insights into the performance of your messages, including metrics such as delivery rates, open rates, and response rates. You will be able to identify areas in which you need to improve and make decisions based on the data in order to maximize the effectiveness of your SMS marketing campaigns if you analyze this data.

Conclusion

In conclusion, short message service (SMS) marketing is an effective tool that companies can use to reach and engage their target audience. You can create successful SMS marketing campaigns that drive engagement and conversions by building your SMS marketing list, creating effective SMS messages, timing your SMS messages, and measuring the performance of your SMS marketing. In the following chapters, we will investigate the various approaches to mobile marketing that are available, as well as discuss how to apply these approaches successfully to SMS marketing.

Chapter 11: Maximizing Mobile Email Marketing Campaigns

The use of mobile email marketing by businesses is a powerful tool that can engage their audience and drive conversions. It is absolutely necessary to optimize your email marketing campaigns for mobile devices in light of the fact that the majority of emails are now opened on mobile devices. In this chapter, we will discuss how to get the most out of your mobile email marketing campaigns so that you can achieve your desired outcomes.

Getting a Handle on Mobile and Email Marketing

Sending email messages to your audience through a mobile device with the intention of promoting your business or products, sharing updates and news, or providing valuable content to your subscribers is an example of mobile email marketing.

It is essential to optimize your email marketing campaigns for mobile devices in this day and age, given the proliferation of mobile devices, in order to maintain audience engagement and increase conversions. Mobile email marketing entails the creation of email designs that are responsive, meaning that they adjust to different screen sizes, as well as the use of compelling visuals and messaging in order to capture the attention of your audience.

Adapting the Design of Your Emails to Be Read on Mobile Devices

Optimizing your email design for mobile devices is essential for engaging your audience and driving conversions. Your email design should be responsive, meaning that the layout should change to accommodate a variety of screen sizes and resolutions.

If you want to make it simple for users to interact with your email, you should think about employing a layout with a single column, clear and succinct messaging, and an obvious call to action (CTA). Make your email more visually appealing and engaging by incorporating different types of visual elements, such as images and videos.

Creating Content That Will Captivate Your Email Readers

It is essential to create compelling content for your emails if you want to engage your audience and increase conversions. It is important that the content of your emails is pertinent to your audience and offers them something of value.

To make your email more interesting and engaging for the recipient, use messaging that is clear and concise, effectively communicates your message, and incorporates visual elements such as images and videos. Take into consideration personalizing the content of your emails in order to make it more pertinent to your audience and compelling to read.

Organizing and Classifying Your Email List

It is essential to segment your email list in order to create email marketing campaigns that are relevant and targeted. You can create targeted email campaigns that are more likely to resonate with your audience if you segment your email list based on demographic, behavioral, and preference data. This can be accomplished by segmenting your email list.

If you want to create targeted campaigns that have a better chance of driving conversions, you should think about segmenting your email list based on characteristics such as age, gender, location, interests, and previous purchasing behavior.

Evaluation of the Effectiveness of Your Email Marketing

It is absolutely necessary to measure the performance of your email marketing in order to ensure the success of your email marketing campaigns. You can determine what is successful and what is not in your email marketing strategy by tracking metrics such as the percentage of recipients who open your emails, the percentage of recipients who click through to your website, and the percentage of recipients who convert.

Email marketing platforms such as Mailchimp and Constant Contact provide valuable insights into your email marketing performance. These insights can include metrics such as open rates, click-through rates, and conversion rates. You will be able to identify areas in which you need to improve as well as make decisions driven by the data in order to optimize your email marketing campaigns if you analyze this data.

Conclusion

To summarize, in order to get the most out of your mobile email marketing campaigns, you need to carefully plan and carry them out. You can create successful email marketing campaigns that drive engagement and conversions by optimizing your email design for mobile devices, crafting compelling email content, segmenting your email list, and measuring the performance of your email marketing. In the following chapters, we will investigate the various approaches to mobile marketing that are available, as well as discuss how to apply these approaches successfully to email marketing.

Chapter 12: Creating Compelling Mobile Content

In order for businesses to successfully engage their audience and drive conversions, it is essential for them to create compelling mobile content. It is essential to optimize your content for mobile viewing in this day and age of the proliferation of mobile devices and to produce content that strikes a chord with your audience. In this chapter, we will discuss how to create compelling content for mobile devices, with the end goal of increasing user engagement and conversions.

Understanding Mobile Content

Text, images, videos, and even social media posts can all be considered mobile content as long as they are formatted in a way that is suitable for viewing on a mobile device. It is essential to create content that is optimized for mobile viewing and engages your audience in this day and age because of the proliferation of mobile devices.

Developing Text Content That Is Captivating

It is essential to develop compelling text content if you want to engage your audience and increase the number of conversions you see. The content of your text should be understandable and to the point, with messaging that strikes a chord with your audience.

To make your content easier to read and scan, you might want to think about incorporating headlines and subheadings. In order to make your content more visually appealing and to break up large blocks of text, you should make use of visual elements such as images and infographics.

Creating Engaging Visual Content

It is essential to create visually engaging content if you want to be successful in capturing the attention of your audience and driving engagement. Images, infographics, videos, and other visual elements that are formatted specifically for mobile viewing make up what is known as "visual content."

Make use of high-quality images and videos that are pertinent to the content you're providing and that resonate with your audience. If you want to create visually appealing graphics and infographics that make your content more engaging, you might want to think about using tools such as Canva or Adobe Spark.

Developing Content That Is Interactive

Developing content that users can interact with is an effective strategy for engaging an audience and providing a more tailored experience for users. The term "interactive content" refers to content such as quizzes, polls, surveys, and other items that give users the opportunity to interact with the content you provide.

When writing content for your blog or social media accounts, you might want to think about including interactive elements like polls and quizzes so that you can increase user engagement and offer a more personalized experience to your audience.

Assessing the Effectiveness of Your Content

It is absolutely essential to the success of your content marketing campaigns that you measure the performance of your content. You will be able to determine what aspects of your content marketing strategy are successful and what aspects need improvement if you track metrics such as the number of conversions, shares, and engagements.

Tools for content analytics such as Google Analytics and Hootsuite Insights give you valuable insights into the performance of your content, including metrics such as engagement, shares, and conversions. You will be able to identify areas in which you need to improve as well as make decisions driven by the data in order to optimize your content marketing campaigns if you analyze this data.

Conclusion

In conclusion, developing compelling content for mobile devices is an absolute necessity if you want to engage your audience and drive conversions. You can create successful content marketing campaigns that drive engagement and conversions by creating text content that is compelling, visual content that is engaging, and interactive content and then measuring how well each of these types of content performs. In the following chapters, we will investigate the numerous approaches to mobile marketing that are available, as well as discuss how to apply these approaches successfully to content marketing.

Chapter 13: Harnessing the Potential of Mobile Social Media

Platforms for social media communication such as Facebook, Twitter, and Instagram have emerged as indispensable components of the mobile marketing mix. It is essential for businesses to optimize their social media marketing campaigns for mobile viewing as the majority of social media users access platforms through their mobile devices. In the following chapter, we will discuss how to make the most of the opportunities presented by mobile social media for your company.

Acquiring Knowledge of Mobile Social Media

Utilizing social media platforms on mobile devices allows you to promote your company or products, share updates and news, and engage with your audience. Mobile social media can also be referred to as mobile marketing. Because of the proliferation of mobile devices, social media has evolved into an instrument that is absolutely necessary for companies in order to interact with their target audience and generate conversions.

Implementing Mobile-Friendly Optimization Into Your Social Media Strategy

When it comes to engaging your audience and driving conversions with social media, optimizing your strategy for mobile devices is absolutely necessary. The creation of content that is optimized for viewing on mobile devices and that incorporates visual elements such as images and videos ought to be an integral part of your social media strategy.

Take into consideration the use of vertical video or image content for platforms such as TikTok and Instagram, which are optimized for viewing on mobile devices. Create visually appealing graphics and infographics that make your content more engaging by using tools like Canva or Adobe Spark. These tools allow you to create visually appealing graphics and infographics.

Participating in Conversations with Your Social Media Followers

Building relationships and increasing conversions both require active participation from your social media audience, which is essential. Platforms for social media provide a one-of-a-kind opportunity to engage with one's audience in real time and to provide a personalized experience for one's users.

You should think about replying to comments and messages in a timely manner and using social media listening tools to monitor mentions of your brand and conversations pertaining to your company. Use contests and giveaways on social media to encourage users to engage with your content and drive conversions.

Increasing Users of Your Social Media Accounts Through Mobile Marketing

It is essential to promote your social media accounts on mobile devices if you want to grow your audience and increase engagement with your content. You should think about promoting your social media accounts on your website, in your email marketing campaigns, and in any other marketing materials you use.

You can also use advertisements on social media platforms to reach a specific audience and attract followers to your social media profiles. You can promote your social media accounts and provide context and background information by telling stories and posting content on social media.

Assessing How Well You Are Performing on Social Media

It is absolutely essential to measure your performance on social media if you want your social media marketing campaigns to be successful. You can determine what aspects of your social media marketing strategy are successful and what aspects are not by tracking metrics such as engagement, the number of followers, and conversions. You can then adjust your strategy accordingly.

Insights into your social media performance, such as engagement, followers, and conversions, can be gleaned from social media analytics tools such as Facebook Insights and Twitter Analytics. These tools provide valuable insights into your social media performance. You will be able to identify areas in which you need to improve and make decisions based on the data in order to maximize the effectiveness of your social media marketing campaigns if you analyze this data.

Conclusion

In conclusion, mobile social media is a powerful tool for businesses to engage their audience and drive conversions in order to increase revenue. You can create successful social media marketing campaigns that generate engagement and conversions by optimizing your social media strategy for mobile devices, engaging with your social media audience, promoting your social media accounts on mobile devices, and measuring your social media performance. In the following chapters, we will investigate the numerous approaches to mobile marketing that exist, as well as discuss how social media marketers can make effective use of these approaches.

Chapter 14: The Benefits of Mobile Coupons and Promotions

Businesses have a powerful tool at their disposal in the form of mobile coupons and promotions that can drive sales and engage their audience. Mobile coupons and promotions have emerged as an essential component of the mobile marketing mix in recent years thanks to the proliferation of mobile devices. In the following section, we will discuss the ways in which your company can benefit from utilizing mobile coupons and promotions.

An increase in revenue

Increasing sales for your company with the help of mobile coupons and promotions is possible. You can increase the number of people who make a purchase from your audience and convert them into customers by providing them with access to special discounts and sales.

Think about offering time-sensitive discounts and specials to generate a sense of urgency among your target audience and encourage them to make a purchase. Rewarding loyal customers and cultivating relationships with your audience can be accomplished through the use of mobile coupons and promotions.

More Extensive Coverage

Coupons and promotions that can be used on mobile devices have a wider reach than those that can only be printed out. Mobile coupons and promotions can be easily shared and redeemed through social media, email, and other digital channels. This is made possible by the fact that the majority of people now have mobile devices in their possession.

It may be beneficial to include mobile coupons and promotions in your social media marketing campaigns as well as your email marketing campaigns in order to attract a larger audience. Reaching a targeted audience and driving conversions can be accomplished through the use of social media ads and targeted email marketing.

a higher level of participation

Increasing audience engagement with your brand can be accomplished with the help of mobile coupons and promotions. You can generate a sense of excitement among your audience and provide an incentive for them to interact with your company by providing them with access to special discounts and promotions.

You might want to think about incorporating mobile coupons and promotions into your social media marketing campaigns as well as your email marketing campaigns in order to encourage engagement with your audience. Make use of activities such as contests and giveaways to generate excitement, as well as to encourage participation.

Cost-effective

Coupons and promotions that can be used on mobile devices are an efficient and inexpensive way to drive sales and engage your audience. Mobile coupons and promotions, in comparison to traditional coupons and promotions, can be easily created and distributed through digital channels.

Think about lowering your marketing expenses and increasing revenue by offering mobile coupons and promotions to customers. Make the process of creating and distributing mobile coupons and promotions more manageable by utilizing tools such as coupon creator or Textedly.

Measurable Results

Mobile coupons and promotions offer measurable results, which enables you to track the effectiveness of your campaigns and make decisions based on data to optimize your mobile marketing strategy. These results can be obtained through the use of mobile coupons and promotions.

Think about making use of tracking applications such as Google Analytics or Hootsuite Insights in order to monitor key performance indicators such as engagement, conversions, and redemption rates. You will be able to identify areas in which you need to improve as well as make decisions driven by the data in order to optimize your mobile marketing campaigns if you analyze this data.

Conclusion

In conclusion, mobile coupons and promotions are a powerful tool for businesses to drive sales and engage their audience. This is because they can be sent directly to customers' mobile devices. You can incentivize your audience to make a purchase and build relationships with your customers by providing them with special discounts and promotions that are only available to them. Mobile coupons and promotions can help increase your reach, drive engagement, and provide measurable results. Other benefits include increased reach. In the following chapters, we will investigate the numerous approaches to mobile marketing that are available, as well as the most efficient ways to apply these approaches when creating mobile coupons and running mobile promotions.

Chapter 15: Building a Strong Mobile Website

It is absolutely necessary to have an effective mobile website in order to engage your audience and increase conversions. It is absolutely necessary to optimize your website for mobile viewing as the majority of internet users are now accessing websites through their mobile devices. In this chapter, we will discuss how to construct an effective mobile website that keeps your audience engaged and propels conversions.

Responsive Design

When developing a powerful mobile website, you absolutely need to use a design that is responsive. Your website's layout and content will be automatically adjusted by a responsive design so that it will look good on any device, regardless of the screen size. This will make it much simpler to navigate and read on mobile devices.

You should give some thought to utilizing a mobile-first design approach, which puts an emphasis on the quality of the mobile experience and guarantees that your website is suitable for use on mobile devices. To make it easy for users to interact with your website, use a design that is uncluttered and straightforward, along with messaging that is direct and to the point, and a prominent call to action.

Quick Times to Load

When developing a powerful mobile website, having quick load times is absolutely necessary. Mobile users have come to expect that websites will load quickly, and slow load times can contribute to high bounce rates as well as a negative user experience.

You should give some thought to optimizing your website for quick load times by reducing the file sizes of images and videos, compressing files, and making use of caching tools. This will help reduce load times.

Test the load times of your website with applications like Google's PageSpeed Insights or GTmetrix to determine the areas in which you could stand to make improvements.

Uncomplicated Steering

A mobile website needs to have navigation that is easy to understand in order to be successful. Mobile users have high expectations that websites will be simple to navigate and provide quick access to the information they require.

It is important to make it simple for users to find the information they require, so you should think about utilizing a navigation menu that is both clear and succinct, with labels that are simple to understand and dropdown menus. Make it simple for users to locate the information or products they are looking for by providing a search bar on your website.

Improved and Enhanced Content

It is essential to have content that has been optimized in order to develop a successful mobile website. Users of mobile devices anticipate that websites will be simple to read and navigate, and will feature content that has been formatted specifically for viewing on mobile devices.

You should think about using messaging that is clear and concise, which effectively communicates your message, and incorporates visual elements such as images and videos in order to make your website more engaging. Make your content easier to read and scan by breaking up large blocks of text with bullet points and subheadings. This will make your content more readable.

Forms Optimized for Mobile Devices

For a mobile website to be successful, it must have forms that are compatible with mobile devices. Users of mobile devices have come to expect that forms should be simple to complete and submit on their devices.

If you want to reduce the number of steps necessary to finish filling out the form, you should think about using forms that are straightforward, uncomplicated, and easy to complete. Make it simple for users to fill out the form in a short amount of time by incorporating autocomplete features and populating fields with information they have previously provided.

Assessing the Effectiveness of Your Website

It is essential to measure the performance of your website if you want your mobile website to be successful. You'll be able to determine what aspects of your mobile marketing strategy are successful and which ones aren't if you track metrics such as bounce rates, click-through rates, and conversion rates. You can then adapt your strategy as necessary.

When it comes to tracking metrics such as bounce rates, click-through rates, and conversion rates, you might want to think about using tools such as Google Analytics or Hotjar. You will be able to determine the areas of your mobile website that require improvement after conducting an analysis of this data and then basing your decision-making on the findings of that analysis.

Conclusion

To summarize, developing an effective mobile website is critical to engaging your audience and increasing conversions. You can create a successful mobile website that engages your audience and drives conversions by using a responsive design, optimizing your content, using clear navigation, and mobile-friendly forms, and measuring the performance of your website. In the following chapters, we will examine a variety of mobile marketing strategies, as well as discuss how to implement these strategies in an efficient manner for mobile websites.

Chapter 16: Mobile Analytics and Metrics

The success of your mobile marketing campaigns is inextricably linked to the analytics and metrics collected from mobile devices. You can determine what aspects of your mobile marketing strategy are successful and what aspects are not by tracking metrics such as engagement, conversion rates, and click-through rates. You can then adapt your strategy accordingly. In the following chapter, we will discuss mobile analytics and metrics, as well as how to make effective use of them for your mobile marketing campaigns.

Defining Mobile Metrics

Mobile metrics are data points that are used to measure how successful your mobile marketing campaigns have been. Metrics such as clicks, impressions, and bounce rates can be considered engagement metrics. Click-through rates and conversion rates can be considered conversion metrics. Revenue metrics such as sales and return on investment can be considered revenue metrics.

Think about defining your mobile metrics based on the objectives you want to achieve with your mobile marketing, such as increasing the number of conversions or engagements. Tracking and analyzing your mobile metrics, as well as locating areas in which you can make improvements, can be accomplished with the assistance of tracking and analysis tools such as Google Analytics and Adobe Analytics.

Engagement Metrics

Metrics that measure engagement provide insight into the degree to which an audience participates in mobile marketing efforts. Metrics of engagement can include clicks, impressions, and bounce rates, among other things.

Think about keeping track of your engagement metrics in order to figure out how your audience interacts with the mobile marketing campaigns you run. You can identify areas in which you need to improve your mobile marketing strategy by utilizing engagement metrics, such as making improvements to the design of your website or producing content that is more engaging.

Metrics Regarding Conversions

Your mobile marketing campaigns' ability to successfully drive conversions is evaluated using metrics known as conversion metrics. Click-through rates and conversion rates are two examples of the types of metrics that can be considered conversion metrics.

Consider keeping track of your conversion metrics to determine how effectively your mobile marketing campaigns are bringing in new customers. Utilize conversion metrics to help you identify areas of your mobile marketing strategy that need to be optimized, such as improving the design of your mobile website or developing mobile ads that are more effective.

Revenue Metrics

Your mobile marketing campaigns' ability to successfully generate revenue for your company can be evaluated using metrics known as revenue metrics. Metrics regarding revenue can consist of sales as well as return on investment.

Consider keeping track of your revenue metrics to evaluate the effectiveness of your mobile marketing campaigns in terms of generating revenue. You can determine areas in which you need to improve your mobile marketing strategy by using revenue metrics. For example, you could improve your mobile e-commerce strategy or create more effective mobile promotions.

Testing on A and B

Testing with the A/B method is an effective method for improving the performance of mobile marketing campaigns. The purpose of A/B testing is to determine which variant of a mobile marketing campaign is more successful by comparing the results of testing two distinct versions of the campaign.

When trying to improve the effectiveness of your mobile marketing campaigns, consider using A/B testing. You can improve your mobile marketing strategy by using A/B testing to compare different versions of your mobile advertisements, mobile website design, or mobile promotions to determine which version is more successful and to make decisions based on the data collected.

Mobile Attribution

Mobile attribution refers to the process of giving credit for a mobile conversion to the various touchpoints that were involved in the sale of a mobile device. Understanding which mobile marketing campaigns and channels are responsible for driving conversions and revenue can be facilitated with the help of mobile attribution.

If you want to track how successful your mobile marketing campaigns are, you should think about using mobile attribution. Utilize mobile attribution to determine which channels and campaigns are driving conversions, and then adjust your mobile marketing strategy to reflect those findings.

Conclusion

For your mobile marketing campaigns to be successful, mobile analytics and metrics are absolutely necessary. You can identify areas in which you need to improve your mobile marketing strategy and make decisions driven by data to optimize your mobile marketing campaigns if you track engagement metrics, conversion metrics, and revenue metrics, use A/B testing, and employ mobile attribution. In the following chapters, we will investigate the various approaches to mobile marketing that are available, as well as discuss how to apply these approaches successfully to mobile analytics and metrics.

Chapter 17: The Role of Mobile Influencers in Marketing Campaigns

Mobile marketing campaigns now routinely incorporate mobile influencers as an essential component. Businesses have a better chance of reaching their ideal customers and gaining their audience's trust if they form partnerships with mobile influencers. We are going to discuss the function of mobile influencers in marketing campaigns as well as the most efficient way to make use of them in this chapter.

What exactly does "Mobile Influencer" mean?

A person is considered to be a mobile influencer if they have a sizable and active following on mobile social media platforms such as Instagram, Twitter, and TikTok. Mobile influencers have the ability to sway their audience's purchasing decisions because of their audience's high level of trust in them.

You should give some thought to locating mobile industry influencers who are compatible with the values of your brand and your intended audience. Find popular mobile influencers with the help of tools like Hootsuite Insights and BuzzSumo, then examine the engagement metrics that those influencers generate.

Advantages to Utilizing Mobile Influencers

The use of mobile influencers in your mobile marketing campaigns can have a number of advantageous effects. Businesses have a better chance of reaching their ideal customers and gaining their audience's trust if they form partnerships with mobile influencers.

Think about forming a partnership with mobile influencers in order to raise the profile of your brand, increase the number of conversions, and establish trust with your target audience. Utilize mobile influencers as a means of promoting your products or services and producing content that is both authentic and engaging in order to achieve maximum resonance with your target audience.

Different Categories of Mobile Media Influencers

There are numerous categories of mobile influencers, such as micro-influencers, macro-influencers, and celebrity influencers. Micro-influencers are the smallest of these categories.

Micro-influencers are people who have a smaller following but a significant amount of interaction with that audience. Micro-influencers have the potential to attract a more specific audience and inspire a higher level of trust among their followers.

Macro-influencers have a much larger number of followers, but they may have less interaction with those followers. Your brand can get more exposure and access to a wider audience when macro-influencers are involved.

The most popular influencers are celebrities, but it's possible that they don't provide the same level of engagement or trust with their audience. A high level of exposure and awareness can be generated for your brand through the use of celebrity influencers.

You should think about identifying the type of mobile influencer that aligns with the objectives of your mobile marketing and the audience you are trying to reach. Identify popular mobile influencers in your industry by using tools such as Hopper HQ or Influencer.co, and then analyze the engagement metrics that these influencers generate.

Finding the Right Influencer for Your Mobile Device

It is absolutely essential to the success of your mobile marketing campaigns that you select the appropriate mobile influencer. When selecting a mobile influencer, it is important to take into account the demographics of their audience, the engagement metrics they use, and their authenticity.

Think about forming a partnership with mobile influencers whose values and audience are compatible with those of your brand. Make use of applications such as Hootsuite Insights or BuzzSumo to perform an analysis of the engagement metrics of mobile influencers and determine which individuals have high levels of both engagement and authenticity.

Collaboration with Mobile Industry Influencers

Creating a partnership that is mutually beneficial for both your brand and the mobile influencer is required when working with mobile influencers. When working with mobile influencers, you should think about developing a clear partnership agreement that outlines your expectations and the deliverables that are expected from you.

Think about forming strategic alliances with mobile influencers so that you can produce content that is both authentic and engaging and that will resonate with your audience. Employ mobile influencers to promote your goods or services and earn the audience's trust so you can move forward with your business goals.

Assessing the Level of Success Achieved by Mobile Influencer Campaigns

It is essential to the success of your mobile marketing strategy that you measure the effectiveness of the mobile influencer campaigns you run. You'll be able to determine what aspects of your mobile marketing strategy are successful and what aspects need improvement if you track metrics such as user engagement, the number of conversions, and revenue.

It is recommended that you track the success of your mobile influencer campaigns by utilizing applications such as Google Analytics or Hootsuite Insights. Make decisions that are informed by the data you collect using metrics such as engagement rates, click-through rates, and conversion rates to improve your mobile influencer marketing campaigns. This will help you identify areas in which you need to make improvements.

Conclusion

To summarize, mobile influencers have developed into an indispensable component of mobile marketing campaigns. Businesses have a better chance of reaching their ideal customers and gaining their audience's trust if they form partnerships with mobile influencers.

Chapter 18: Utilizing Artificial Intelligence for Mobile Marketing

The way in which businesses approach mobile marketing has been fundamentally altered by artificial intelligence (AI). Automating processes, personalizing content, and optimizing marketing campaigns are all possible for businesses that use artificial intelligence. In this chapter, we will discuss how to make use of artificial intelligence (AI) for mobile marketing, as well as how to make effective use of it.

What exactly does "artificial intelligence" refer to?

The simulation of human intelligence processes by computer systems is what we mean when we talk about artificial intelligence. AI systems are able to perform data analysis, recognize patterns in the data, and base decisions on the data alone.

If you want better results from your campaigns, you should think about using AI to automate processes, personalize content, and optimize them.

Advantages to Be Obtained from Employing AI in Mobile Marketing

Using AI for mobile marketing can provide several benefits for businesses. Automating processes, personalizing content, and optimizing marketing campaigns are all possible for businesses that use artificial intelligence.

Think about using AI to find patterns in the data you have, to personalize your content for the people who will be viewing it, and to improve the results of your marketing campaigns.

Strategies for Implementing AI in Mobile Marketing

There are many different applications of AI in mobile marketing, including the following:

The term "predictive analytics" refers to the process of analyzing data, as well as using statistical algorithms and machine learning methods, in order to recognize patterns and make forecasts about future events.

Think about using predictive analytics in order to recognize patterns in the actions of your audience and to make forecasts about future results, such as conversion rates or the percentage of customers who churn out.

Chatbots: Chatbots automate customer interactions and provide personalized customer service by utilizing techniques such as natural language processing and machine learning. Chatbots are also known as conversational interfaces.

You might want to think about implementing chatbots in order to automate your interactions with customers, offer personalized recommendations, and boost customer satisfaction.

The term "personalization" refers to the application of artificial intelligence (AI) to data in order to generate personalized content and recommendations for your audience.

Think about using personalization so that you can provide personalized product recommendations, tailor your messaging to your audience, and increase the percentage of customers who convert as a result of your efforts.

Improve the Results of Your Campaigns by Using AI to Analyze Data and Identify Patterns AI can analyze data and identify patterns to improve the results of your campaigns.

Think about using artificial intelligence to optimize your campaigns so that you can achieve better results, such as higher click-through rates or lower bounce rates.

Assessing the Impact of Artificial Intelligence on Mobile Marketing

It is essential to the success of your mobile marketing strategy that you measure the efficacy of artificial intelligence for mobile marketing. You'll be able to determine what aspects of your mobile marketing strategy are successful and what aspects need improvement if you track metrics such as user engagement, the number of conversions, and revenue.

It is recommended that you track the success of your AI-powered mobile marketing campaigns by making use of applications such as Google Analytics or Adobe Analytics. You can optimize your mobile marketing strategy by using metrics such as click-through rates, engagement rates, and conversion rates to determine the areas in which you need to make improvements and to drive your decision-making process with data.

The Obstacles Faced When Employing AI in Mobile Marketing

The use of artificial intelligence (AI) in mobile marketing can present a number of challenges to businesses. These difficulties include the following:

Data Security: Artificial intelligence systems need access to large amounts of data, which can present some potential security risks.

When thinking about how to protect your data and ensure the safety of your AI systems, you should give some thought to using encrypted methods of data storage and storing.

Implementation: The process of putting AI systems into action can be difficult and calls for specialized knowledge.

You might want to think about collaborating with a group of AI specialists in order to implement your AI systems and ensure that they are effectively integrated into your mobile marketing strategy.

The creation and deployment of AI systems can come at a high financial cost.

Think about creating a budget to cover the costs of developing and implementing your AI systems, and take into account the potential long-term benefits of incorporating AI into your mobile marketing campaigns.

Conclusion

The use of artificial intelligence (AI) in mobile marketing can provide a number of benefits to companies, including the automation of processes, the personalization of content, and the optimization of campaigns for improved results. If you want to provide a better experience for your customers and see better results, you should think about incorporating AI into your mobile marketing strategy. You can determine the success of your AI-powered mobile marketing campaigns by using metrics such as engagement rates, click-through rates, and conversion rates. However, you should be aware of the challenges that are associated with using AI, such as the cost of implementation and concerns about the safety of your data. Businesses are able to take their mobile marketing strategies to the next level and provide a better experience for their customers if they make use of the most recent AI technologies and remain current with the latest trends.

Chapter 19: The Future of Mobile Marketing Trends

Mobile marketing is a dynamic industry that is always adapting to accommodate emerging industry trends and technological advancements. In this chapter, we will take a look at some of the most recent trends in mobile marketing and discuss what these trends could mean for the industry moving forward.

The use of augmented reality.

In recent years, augmented reality, also known as AR, has become increasingly popular, leading to an increase in the number of businesses that are incorporating AR into their mobile marketing strategies. AR makes it possible for companies to provide their customers with immersive experiences, such as the ability to virtually try on different items of clothing or makeup.

Think about incorporating augmented reality (AR) into your mobile marketing strategy so that you can provide your customers with more exciting and memorable experiences and differentiate your brand from those of your rivals.

Voice Reconnaissance

The proliferation of smart speakers such as the Amazon Echo and the Google Home has led to an increase in the utilization of voice search. You can improve your chances of being discovered by people who use voice search if you optimize the content of your mobile site or app for voice searches.

You should think about optimizing your mobile content for voice search by using keywords and phrases that are found naturally in language and by creating content that responds to common questions asked by voice search.

Artificial Intelligence

The use of artificial intelligence (AI) by businesses to automate processes, personalize content, and optimize campaigns for better results has made AI an essential component of mobile marketing.

You should think about using AI to improve the effectiveness of your mobile marketing campaigns and to offer your customers more individualized experiences.

Video Content

Over the past few years, video content has seen a rise in popularity, and as a result, an increasing number of businesses are beginning to incorporate video into their strategies for mobile marketing. Businesses have the ability to capture and keep the attention of their target audience if they produce video content that is both interesting and informative.

Consider integrating video into your mobile marketing strategy so that you can produce content that is both more interesting and informative for your target demographic.

Mobile Payments

The proliferation of mobile wallet applications such as Apple Pay and Google Wallet has contributed to the widespread acceptance of mobile payments. You can make it simpler for your customers to make purchases while they are on the move by including mobile payments as part of the mobile marketing strategy you employ.

You might want to think about incorporating mobile payments into your mobile marketing strategy so that you can offer your customers a shopping experience that is more convenient and hassle-free.

Personalization

The use of data and AI by businesses to create more personalized experiences for their customers has resulted in the rise of personalization as an increasingly important aspect of mobile marketing. Businesses have the opportunity to strengthen their relationships with their customers and improve customer loyalty by providing personalized recommendations and content to those customers.

You might want to think about incorporating personalization into your mobile marketing strategy by making use of data and AI to generate personalized content and recommendations for your clientele.

Chatbots

In recent years, chatbots have seen a rise in popularity, and an increasing number of companies are employing them in order to automate their interactions with customers and to provide a more individualized level of customer service.

You might want to think about incorporating chatbots into your mobile marketing strategy so that you can automate your interactions with customers, as well as provide more personalized recommendations and assistance.

Social Media

The use of social media by businesses in order to communicate with and attract the attention of their target demographic has made social media an essential component of mobile marketing. Businesses are able to attract and keep the attention of their ideal customers by publishing content on social media platforms that is both interesting and educational.

You should give some thought to incorporating social media into your mobile marketing strategy in order to reach and engage with your target audience, as well as to build stronger relationships with your customers.

In conclusion, the future of trends in mobile marketing is one that is always shifting, with new trends and technologies appearing all the time. Businesses have the ability to enhance their mobile marketing strategies and provide an improved experience for their customers if they maintain a current awareness of the most recent developments in mobile marketing technologies and trends. If you want to stay ahead of the competition and differentiate your brand in the market, you should think about incorporating some of these newest trends, such as augmented reality, voice search, and personalization, into your mobile marketing strategy.

Chapter 20: Mobile Marketing Best Practices and Techniques

In the following chapter, we will discuss some of the most effective strategies and procedures for mobile marketing. Businesses are able to enhance their mobile marketing strategies and provide a more positive experience for their customers if they put into practice the best practices and techniques currently available.

Learn Your Target Market

When it comes to mobile marketing, knowing your target demographic is one of the most essential best practices there is. You will be able to create content and campaigns that are more personalized and relevant to your audience if you understand the needs and preferences of that audience.

Think about gaining insights into the behavior, preferences, and requirements of your audience through the use of data and analytics. Make use of this information to create content and campaigns that are more personalized for your audience and that resonate with them.

Optimize Your Website for Mobile Devices

Because more and more people are accessing the internet through their mobile devices, it is critical for companies to ensure that their websites are compatible with mobile platforms. This entails the creation of websites that are simple to navigate, load in a reasonable amount of time, and offer a streamlined user experience when viewed on mobile devices.

You should give some thought to using responsive design in order to make sure that your website is optimized for all different types of screens and mobile devices. You can determine the areas of your website's mobile optimization in which you need to make improvements by employing tools such as Google's Mobile-Friendly Test.

Make astute use of text message marketing.

The use of short message service (SMS) marketing can be an efficient way to communicate with and connect with one's target audience. However, it is imperative to use SMS marketing strategically and refrain from spamming your audience with an excessive amount of messages.

You should think about using short message service (SMS) marketing to provide your audience with content that is personalized and relevant to them, such as exclusive promotions or special offers. You can ensure that you are targeting the appropriate audience with the appropriate messages by using segmentation to help you narrow down your options.

Utilize Social Media

The use of social media can be an efficient method of communicating with and connecting with one's target audience. Businesses have the ability to build stronger relationships with their customers if they create content that is both engaging and informative. This allows the businesses to both attract and keep the attention of their target audience.

You might want to think about utilizing social media to share content that is pertinent and informative, engage with your audience, and build awareness of your brand. Utilize social media analytics to monitor the efficacy of your social media marketing campaigns and inform your decision-making in order to fine-tune your social media marketing strategy.

Incorporate Video Content

Over the past few years, video content has seen a rise in popularity, and as a result, an increasing number of businesses are beginning to incorporate video into their strategies for mobile marketing. Businesses have the ability to capture and keep the attention of their target audience if they produce video content that is both interesting and informative.

Consider integrating video into your mobile marketing strategy so that you can produce content that is both more interesting and informative for your target demographic. Create short videos that are simple to watch on mobile devices by utilizing applications such as Instagram Stories or TikTok. These types of applications are designed for mobile use.

Provide Personalized Experiences

The use of data and AI by businesses to create more personalized experiences for their customers has resulted in the rise of personalization as an increasingly important aspect of mobile marketing. Businesses have the opportunity to strengthen their relationships with their customers and improve customer loyalty by providing personalized recommendations and content to those customers.

Think about making use of data and AI to come up with personalized suggestions and content for your customers. You can ensure that you are targeting the appropriate audience with the appropriate messages and that you are creating personalized experiences that resonate with your audience by using segmentation.

Iterate and get better

Testing and optimization are absolutely necessary for the success of mobile marketing. You will be able to determine what aspects of your mobile marketing strategy are working well and what aspects need improvement if you test and optimize your mobile marketing campaigns. Based on this information, you can then make decisions that will help improve your mobile marketing strategy.

Think about putting different aspects of your mobile marketing campaigns, such as ad copy, landing pages, and calls-to-action, through A/B testing to see which ones perform better. Make decisions based on the data you gather from analytics in order to improve your mobile marketing strategy. Use analytics to track the success of your campaigns.

In conclusion, it is essential for businesses to implement best practices and techniques for mobile marketing in order to succeed in the mobile-first world that we live in today. Businesses are able to improve their mobile marketing strategies and provide a better experience for their customers if they gain a better understanding of their target demographic, optimize their websites for mobile devices, make strategic use of SMS marketing, make effective use of social media, incorporate video content, provide personalized customer service, and test and optimize their campaigns.

Chapter 21: Measuring the ROI of Your Mobile Marketing Campaigns

It is absolutely necessary to calculate the return on investment (ROI) of your mobile marketing campaigns in order to gain an understanding of how successful your campaigns are and to make decisions based on data in order to improve your strategy. In the following section, we will discuss some of the best practices for calculating the return on investment (ROI) of your mobile marketing campaigns.

Establish Your Goals and Evaluate Their Progress

It is absolutely necessary to define your goals and metrics for your mobile marketing campaigns before you begin implementing them. This requires you to determine the objectives you wish to accomplish with your campaigns and the criteria by which you will judge their success.

You might want to think about defining your objectives with the help of SMART goals (specific, measurable, achievable, relevant, and time-bound), and you might also want to think about identifying the metrics that you will use to measure your success, such as engagement rates, click-through rates, conversion rates, and revenue generated.

Make use of tracking and analytics tools.

When it comes to measuring the return on investment (ROI) of your mobile marketing campaigns, analytics and tracking tools are absolutely necessary. With the help of these tools, you'll be able to monitor how successful your campaigns are and pinpoint the aspects of your approach that could use some tweaking.

If you want to monitor how well your mobile marketing campaigns are doing, you should think about utilizing tracking and analytics tools such as Google Analytics, Facebook Analytics, or other similar tools. Track important metrics like engagement rates, click-through rates, conversion rates, and revenue generated with the help of these tools.

Determine the Levels of Participation

When calculating the return on investment (ROI) of your mobile marketing campaigns, engagement rates are an essential metric to track. Engagement rates are a measure of the number of people who are interacting with your content and campaigns. They can assist you in determining the areas of your strategy in which you need to make improvements.

When determining how successful your mobile marketing campaigns are, you may want to think about tracking engagement rates such as the number of likes, shares, comments, and clicks. Utilize these metrics to identify areas in which you need to improve your strategy, such as producing content that is more engaging or refining your calls-to-action.

Check the rates of click-throughs.

The click-through rate, also known as CTR, is a metric that determines how many people are clicking on your mobile marketing campaigns and can assist you in determining the areas of your strategy that require improvement.

If you want to measure how successful your mobile marketing campaigns are, you should think about tracking click-through rates. Utilize these metrics to determine the areas of your strategy in which you need to make improvements, such as optimizing your ad copy, improving your landing pages, or targeting the appropriate audience.

Determine the Rates of Conversion.

The conversion rate is a measurement of how many people take a particular action, such as making a purchase or signing up for a newsletter. Conversion rates can assist you in determining the areas of your strategy in which you need to make improvements.

When determining how successful your mobile marketing campaigns are, tracking conversion rates is one metric to consider. Utilize these metrics to determine the areas of your strategy that need improvement, such as improving your call-to-action, optimizing your landing pages, or targeting the appropriate audience.

Determine the Amount of Money That Was Made

The ultimate metric for measuring the return on investment (ROI) of your mobile marketing campaigns is the amount of revenue that is generated. You can gain insight into the efficiency of your marketing campaigns in terms of driving sales and revenue for your company if you monitor and analyze the revenue that is produced by those campaigns.

You might want to measure the success of your mobile marketing campaigns by tracking the amount of revenue they generate. Utilize these metrics to identify areas of your strategy where you need to improve it, such as improving your product offerings, targeting the appropriate audience, or optimizing the process for mobile checkout.

In conclusion, measuring the return on investment (ROI) of your mobile marketing campaigns is essential if you want to gain an understanding of how successful your campaigns are and make decisions based on data in order to improve your strategy. Businesses are able to measure the success of their mobile marketing campaigns and make decisions based on data to improve their strategy if they first define their objectives and metrics, then use analytics and tracking tools, measure engagement rates, click-through rates, conversion rates, and revenue generated, and then compare those results to their objectives and metrics. To measure the return on investment (ROI) of your mobile marketing campaigns and to generate better results for your company, you should think about incorporating these best practices into your mobile marketing strategy.

Chapter 22: Managing Your Mobile Marketing Budget

It is critical that you effectively manage the budget for your mobile marketing efforts if you want to achieve the highest return on investment (ROI) possible from your marketing campaigns. In this chapter, we will discuss some best practices for managing your mobile marketing budget, and we will look at some examples.

Define Your Budget

It is essential to establish your budget before beginning any mobile marketing campaigns before you get started. This requires you to determine how much you are willing to spend on your mobile marketing campaigns as well as how you will distribute your budget across the various channels and campaigns that you will be utilizing.

Think about figuring out the optimal budget for your mobile marketing campaigns by analyzing data and using data visualization tools. Utilize these insights to determine how much of your budget should be allocated to various channels and campaigns, such as advertising on social media platforms, SMS marketing, or mobile app marketing.

Make Use Of Marketing Channels That Are Cost-Effective

When it comes to being a good financial investment, not all types of marketing channels are created equal. If you have a specific audience in mind, specific marketing goals in mind, and a set budget, then certain channels may be more cost-effective than others.

Think about utilizing cost-effective marketing channels, such as advertising on social media, SMS marketing, or email marketing, to reach your target audience and accomplish your marketing goals while staying within your financial means.

Keep an eye on your spending.

It is essential to keep track of your spending in order to ensure that you do not go over your allotted budget and achieve the highest possible return on investment from your mobile marketing campaigns. Monitoring your spending can help you determine the areas in which you need to make adjustments to your budget in order to make your campaigns more effective.

Think about keeping track of your spending with the help of tracking and analytics tools so you can figure out which areas of your budget need to be adjusted. Make use of these insights to improve your campaigns and guarantee that you are getting the highest return on investment (ROI) possible for the money you spend on mobile marketing.

Consider the return on investment.

It is absolutely necessary to concentrate on ROI if you want to make certain that the mobile marketing campaigns you run provide the best possible return on investment. By putting an emphasis on return on investment (ROI), you can determine which aspects of your campaigns require optimization and use data to inform decisions that will help you improve your strategy.

Think about calculating the return on investment (ROI) of your mobile marketing campaigns using data and analytics. Make use of these insights to identify areas in which you need to optimize your campaigns and make decisions based on data to improve your strategy and maximize the return on your investment (ROI).

Iterate and get better

It is essential to test and optimize your mobile marketing campaigns to ensure that you are getting the highest return on investment (ROI) possible for your marketing budget. You will be able to determine what aspects of your campaigns are successful and which need improvement, as well as base your decisions on the data collected, if you test and optimize them.

Think about putting different aspects of your mobile marketing campaigns, such as ad copy, landing pages, and calls-to-action, through A/B testing to see which ones perform better. Make decisions based on the data you gather from analytics in order to improve your mobile marketing strategy. Use analytics to track the success of your campaigns.

Maintain a Current Awareness of Industry Trends

Maintaining a current awareness of developments in your industry is necessary if you want to maintain a lead over your rivals and maximize the return on investment (ROI) you get from your mobile marketing spending. If you keep up with the latest developments in your industry, you'll be in a better position to spot emerging opportunities and fine-tune your approach to stay one step ahead of the competition.

You might want to think about keeping up with the latest trends in the industry by participating in industry events, reading publications related to the industry, and interacting with thought leaders in the mobile marketing industry. Make use of these insights to improve your strategy and stay one step ahead of the other companies in your industry.

In conclusion, if you want to maximize the return on investment (ROI) that your marketing efforts produce, it is imperative that you effectively manage the budget for your mobile marketing efforts. Businesses are able to effectively manage their mobile marketing budgets and obtain the best ROI for their marketing campaigns by keeping up with industry trends, defining their budgets, using marketing channels that are cost-effective, monitoring their spending, concentrating on return on investment (ROI), testing and optimizing their campaigns, and monitoring their spending. You may want to take into consideration incorporating these best practices into your mobile marketing strategy so that you can effectively manage your marketing budget and achieve better results for your company.

Chapter 23: Common Mobile Marketing Mistakes and How to Avoid Them

Mobile marketing has the potential to be an extremely useful instrument for businesses in terms of reaching their intended demographic and accomplishing their marketing goals. However, a significant number of companies continue to commit widespread errors in their mobile marketing, which reduces the efficiency of their campaigns. In this chapter, we will discuss some common errors that are made in mobile marketing, as well as some strategies for avoiding them.

Ignoring Your Target Market as a Whole

Ignoring one's audience is one of the most typical and widespread errors made in mobile marketing. You won't be able to create effective mobile marketing campaigns that resonate with your target audience if you don't have a solid understanding of who that audience is.

To steer clear of this error, make it a priority to conduct thorough research on your intended market and gain an understanding of their expectations, inclinations, and routines. Make use of this information to develop mobile marketing campaigns for your business that speak directly to your target audience, thereby increasing engagement and conversions.

Not Optimizing for Mobile

One more frequent error in mobile marketing is failing to optimize your campaigns for mobile devices. Desktop users have different requirements and habits than mobile users, and if your marketing campaigns aren't optimized for mobile, you could be missing out on valuable engagement and conversions. Mobile users have different requirements and behaviors than desktop users.

Make sure that your mobile marketing campaigns are optimized for mobile devices to ensure that you do not make this common error. This entails utilizing a design that is responsive, layouts that are friendly to mobile devices, and navigation that is simple in order to guarantee that your campaigns are accessible and useful on any mobile device.

Putting an emphasis on quantity rather than quality

Another common mistake made in mobile marketing is placing too much emphasis on quantity over quality. However, this strategy can result in low engagement rates and poor return on investment (ROI). Many companies mistakenly believe that the key to success is to reach as many people as possible with their campaigns.

When it comes to your mobile marketing campaigns, you should prioritize quality over quantity to avoid making the mistake that was just described. This entails selecting the appropriate demographic to target, developing content and messaging of a high standard, and providing individualized experiences that strike a chord with the demographic in question.

ignoring the marketing of mobile applications

Another common mistake made in mobile marketing is neglecting the marketing of mobile applications. Mobile apps have the potential to be an extremely useful tool for businesses in terms of reaching their target audience as well as driving engagement and conversions; however, many businesses are unable to effectively leverage this channel.

If you want to avoid making this mistake, your mobile marketing strategy should seriously consider incorporating mobile app marketing. This entails developing mobile applications that are not only interesting and helpful but also provide your target audience with something of value, and then utilizing mobile app marketing strategies, such as in-app advertising and push notifications, in order to drive engagement and conversions.

Failure to Measure Return on Investment

Another common oversight is failing to measure the return on investment (ROI) of your mobile marketing campaigns. If you don't measure the success of your campaigns, you won't be able to determine the areas in which you need to optimize your strategy in order to improve your return on investment (ROI).

Use analytics and tracking tools to measure the return on investment (ROI) of your mobile marketing campaigns so that you can avoid making this mistake. Make use of these insights to determine the areas in which you need to optimize your strategy and to make decisions based on data in order to improve your return on investment (ROI).

Failure to perform testing and optimization

Another common oversight involves mobile marketing campaigns that aren't properly tested and optimized. Mobile users have different requirements and behaviors than desktop users, and if you don't test and optimize your campaigns, you may be missing out on valuable engagement and conversions. Mobile users have different requirements and behaviors than desktop users.

You can prevent yourself from making this error by utilizing A/B testing to evaluate various aspects of your mobile marketing campaigns, such as ad copy, landing pages, and calls-to-action. Make decisions based on the data you gather from analytics in order to improve your mobile marketing strategy. Use analytics to track the success of your campaigns.

In conclusion, if you want to ensure that your mobile marketing campaigns are successful and that you meet your marketing goals, it is essential to avoid making common mobile marketing mistakes. Businesses are able to steer clear of typical mobile marketing blunders and generate better results for their operations if they understand their target demographic, optimize their websites and content for mobile devices, prioritize quality over quantity, leverage mobile app marketing, measure return on investment, and test and optimize their marketing campaigns. You should give some thought to incorporating these best practices into your mobile marketing strategy in order to avoid making the typical errors that are associated with mobile marketing and to achieve better results for your company.

Chapter 24: Ethical Considerations in Mobile Marketing

Mobile marketing has the potential to be an extremely useful instrument for businesses in terms of reaching their intended demographic and accomplishing their marketing goals. When developing their mobile marketing campaigns, however, businesses need to bear in mind a number of ethical considerations that must be taken into account. In this chapter, we will discuss some ethical considerations that should be taken into account when engaging in mobile marketing.

Transparency

When it comes to mobile marketing, transparency is absolutely necessary. Businesses have a responsibility to be open and honest about the information they obtain from their customers and the ways in which they put that information to use in mobile marketing efforts.

Businesses should provide users with privacy policies that are easy to understand and that inform users about the data they collect as well as how they use this data in order to ensure transparency. Users should be given the option to opt out of their data being collected and used by companies, and companies should make this option available.

Marketing that Is Done With People's Consent

Another ethical consideration that should be made in mobile marketing is marketing based on permission. Before sending users marketing messages or collecting their data, companies are required to obtain permission from those users first.

When collecting user data or sending out marketing messages, companies should give customers easy-to-understand and direct opt-in choices so that they can engage in marketing that is based on prior approval. Additionally, users should be given the option to opt out of receiving marketing messages and having their data collected by companies.

Maintaining the Confidentiality of Users

Mobile marketing must be conducted with the utmost regard for the privacy of its users. Businesses have a responsibility to protect the privacy of their users and to make certain that their mobile marketing efforts do not in any way violate the privacy of their customers.

Businesses have a responsibility to their customers to protect their privacy by limiting the information they collect about customers to only that which is required for their marketing efforts. Additionally, companies have a responsibility to ensure that the data of their customers is kept safe and is not disclosed to outside parties without the customers' prior consent.

Honesty

Honesty is an additional factor to consider when it comes to mobile marketing ethics. When promoting their products or services via mobile devices, companies must conduct themselves in an ethical manner and steer clear of deceptive or misleading advertising.

In order to maintain a trustworthy reputation, companies should make sure that the information contained in their marketing messages is both accurate and honest. When a company makes a claim or statement, they should be careful not to overstate the benefits of their products or services and should provide disclosures that are easy to understand and to the point.

Allowing Users to Make Their Own Choices

In mobile marketing, it is essential to show respect for the choices made by users. Businesses have a responsibility to honor the preferences of their customers and give them the opportunity to decline receiving promotional communications and participate in data collection.

When collecting users' data or sending them marketing messages, companies should give users unambiguous and direct ways to opt out of having their information collected or received. This will ensure that their choices are respected. Additionally, businesses have a responsibility to respect the preferences of users who opt-out of receiving marketing communications and should refrain from sending those users any further promotional messages.

Avoiding Harm

Mobile marketing involves a number of ethical considerations, one of which is preventing harm. Businesses have a responsibility to ensure that the mobile marketing campaigns they run do not harm either the people who use their services or the communities in which they operate.

Businesses should avoid marketing products or services that are harmful to their customers or the communities in which they operate in order to protect themselves and their customers from potential harm. In addition, companies should steer clear of employing any marketing strategies that could be construed as exploitative or deceptive.

To summarize, ethical considerations are absolutely necessary when it comes to mobile marketing. During mobile marketing campaigns, companies are required to avoid causing harm to customers, be honest, be transparent, obtain permission, respect user privacy, and respect the user's right to make choices. Businesses are able to create mobile marketing campaigns that are successful, trustworthy, and respectful of their users and communities if they adhere to the ethical considerations that have been outlined here. To ensure that your mobile marketing campaigns are both ethical and successful, you should think about incorporating the following ethical considerations into your overall strategy.

Chapter 25: Mobile Mastery: Tips and Tricks for Becoming a Mobile Marketing Pro

To become an expert in mobile marketing, it will take you some time, effort, and a commitment to ongoing education and improvement. In this chapter, we will discuss some advice and suggestions that can help you become an expert in mobile marketing.

Maintain Your Awareness of the Latest Trends in Mobile Marketing

If you want to become an expert in mobile marketing, it is absolutely necessary for you to keep up with the latest trends in the field. Mobile marketing is in a state of constant evolution; therefore, it is essential for the development of successful campaigns to remain current on the most recent mobile marketing trends and best practices.

Follow thought leaders and influencers on social media, subscribe to industry publications and blogs, attend industry conferences and events, and read industry publications and blogs to keep up with the latest mobile marketing trends.

Maintain a Constant Focus on Testing and Improving Your Campaigns

In order to become an expert in mobile marketing, it is necessary to conduct ongoing testing and optimization. Testing and optimizing your campaigns is essential for identifying areas for improvement and driving better results. Mobile users have different needs and behaviors than desktop users, and testing and optimizing your campaigns is essential for this reason.

A/B testing allows you to compare two versions of an element of your campaign, such as an advertisement's copy, a landing page, or a call to action. This allows you to continuously test and optimize your campaigns. Make decisions based on the data you gather from analytics in order to improve your mobile marketing strategy. Use analytics to track the success of your campaigns.

Build a Powerful Reputation for Your Mobile Brand

Building a solid mobile brand is absolutely necessary if you want to become an expert in mobile marketing. A powerful mobile brand can help your business to differentiate itself in a crowded market, earn the trust of the people you are trying to reach, and increase user engagement and sales.

To build a powerful mobile brand, you must first define the identity and messaging of your brand, create a website and landing pages that are optimized for mobile use, and use branding that is consistent across all of your mobile marketing channels.

Take Advantage of Mobile Video's Power and Potential

To become an expert in mobile marketing, mobile video is a potent tool that you should utilize. Video content is extremely popular among mobile users, and including mobile video in your marketing efforts can help you increase user engagement and conversion rates.

To take advantage of the power that mobile video offers, you need to produce high-quality video content that addresses your target audience specifically and provides value. Make use of video formats that are compatible with mobile devices, such as vertical video, and optimize the video content you create for mobile devices.

Make use of personalization in order to boost engagement.

The use of personalization is yet another powerful tool that can help one become an expert in mobile marketing. You will be able to create more meaningful and engaging experiences for your target audience with the help of personalization, which will ultimately drive higher engagement and conversion rates.

Collecting data from your users and using that data to deliver personalized experiences, such as personalized messaging, product recommendations, and offers, is one way to use personalization to drive engagement. To do this, collect the data from your users. Make use of marketing automation tools in order to provide these individualized experiences on a large scale.

Conduct Research and Evaluations on Your Various Campaigns

It is absolutely necessary to measure and analyze your campaigns if you want to become an expert in mobile marketing. When it comes to optimizing your strategy, measuring and analyzing your campaigns can help you identify areas that need improvement and make decisions based on the data collected.

Use analytics and tracking tools to track the success of your campaigns in order to measure and analyze the effectiveness of your campaigns. Make use of these insights to determine areas in need of improvement and to make decisions based on data in order to maximize the effectiveness of your mobile marketing strategy.

To summarize, becoming an expert in mobile marketing takes a significant investment of time and effort, as well as a dedication to ongoing education and development. You can become an expert in mobile marketing and get your company better results by keeping up with the latest trends in mobile marketing, continually testing and optimizing your campaigns, developing a powerful mobile brand, leveraging the power of mobile video, using personalization to drive engagement, and measuring and analyzing your campaigns. If you want to become an expert in mobile marketing and drive better results for your company, you should think about how you can incorporate these tips and tricks into your mobile marketing strategy.

Also by B. Vincent

Affiliate Marketing
Affiliate Marketing
Affiliate Marketing

Standalone
Business Employee Discipline
Affiliate Recruiting
Business Layoffs & Firings
Business and Entrepreneur Guide
Business Remote Workforce
Career Transition
Project Management
Precision Targeting
Professional Development
Strategic Planning
Content Marketing
Imminent List Building
Getting Past GateKeepers
Banner Ads
Bookkeeping
Bridge Pages
Business Acquisition

Business Bogging
Business Communication Course
Marketing Automation
Better Meetings
Business Conflict Resolution
Business Culture Course
Conversion Optimization
Creative Solutions
Employee Recruitment
Startup Capital
Employee Incentives
Employee Mentoring
Followership
Servant Leadership
Human Resources
Team Building
Freelancing
Funnel Building
Geo Targeting
Goal Setting
Immanent List Building
Lead Generation
Leadership Course
Leadership Transition
Leadership vs Management
LinkedIn Ads
LinkedIn Marketing
Messenger Marketing
New Management
Newsfeed Ads
Search Ads
Online Learning
Sales Webinars

Side Hustles
Split Testing
Twitter Timeline Advertising
Earning Additional Income Through Side Hustles: Begin Earning
Money Immediately
Making a Living Through Blogging: Earn Money Working From
Home
Create Bonuses for Affiliate Marketing: Your Success Is Encompassed
by Your Bonuses
Internet Marketing Success: The Most Effective Traffic-Driving
Strategies
JV Recruiting: Joint Ventures Partnerships and Affiliates
Secrets to List Building
Step-by-Step Facebook Marketing: Discover How To Create A
Strategy That Will Help You Grow Your Business
Banner Advertising: Traffic Can Be Boosted by Banner Ads
Affiliate Marketing
Improve Your Marketing Strategy with Internet Marketing
Outsourcing Helps You Save Time and Money
Choosing the Right Content and Marketing for Social Media
Make Products That Will Sell
Launching a Product for Affiliate Marketing
Pinterest as a Marketing Tool
Mobile Mastery: The Ultimate Guide to Successful Mobile Marketing
Campaigns

About the Publisher

Accepting manuscripts in the most categories. We love to help people get their words available to the world.

Revival Waves of Glory focus is to provide more options to be published. We do traditional paperbacks, hardcovers, audio books and ebooks all over the world. A traditional royalty-based publisher that offers self-publishing options, Revival Waves provides a very author friendly and transparent publishing process, with President Bill Vincent involved in the full process of your book. Send us your manuscript and we will contact you as soon as possible.

Contact: Bill Vincent at rwgpublishing@yahoo.com

www.ingramcontent.com/pod-product-compliance
Lightning Source LLC
Chambersburg PA
CBHW051057050326
40690CB00006B/756